# THE POWER OF OUR TEAM

## IS EACH INDIVIDUAL MEMBER

Date:        /        /

THINGS TO BE GRATEFUL FOR TODAY

Date:      /      /
_____

_____
_____
_____
_____
_____
_____
_____
_____
_____
_____
_____
_____
_____
_____
_____
_____
_____
_____

## THINGS TO BE GRATEFUL FOR TODAY

*"Believe in miracles but above all believe in yourself!"*

Date:     /     /

_____
_____
_____
_____
_____
_____
_____
_____
_____
_____
_____
_____
_____
_____
_____
_____
_____
_____
_____

## THINGS TO BE GRATEFUL FOR TODAY

*"Let your dreams be as big as your desire to succeed"*

Date:      /      /

_____
_____
_____
_____
_____
_____
_____
_____
_____
_____
_____
_____
_____
_____
_____
_____
_____
_____
_____
_____

## THINGS TO BE GRATEFUL FOR TODAY

Date:     /     /

## THINGS TO BE GRATEFUL FOR TODAY

Date:      /      /

THINGS TO BE GRATEFUL FOR TODAY

> *"Never be afraid to start something new, if you fail it is just temporary, if you believe and persist you will succeed"*

Date:      /      /

THINGS TO BE GRATEFUL FOR TODAY

> *"Your driving force and your power lies within you and the size of your dreams, never give up!"*

Date:     /    /

---
---
---
---
---
---
---
---
---
---
---
---
---
---
---
---
---
---
---
---
---
---
---

## THINGS TO BE GRATEFUL FOR TODAY

> *"Wherever you go, go with all your heart."*
> *- Confucius*

Date:      /      /

_____

_____

_____

_____

_____

_____

_____

_____

_____

_____

_____

_____

_____

_____

_____

_____

_____

## THINGS TO BE GRATEFUL FOR TODAY

# "Never Ever Give Up"

Date:    /    /

_____
_____
_____
_____
_____
_____
_____
_____
_____
_____
_____
_____
_____
_____
_____
_____
_____
_____
_____
_____
_____
_____
_____

## THINGS TO BE GRATEFUL FOR TODAY

Date:        /        /

## THINGS TO BE GRATEFUL FOR TODAY

Date:      /      /

_____
_____
_____
_____
_____
_____
_____
_____
_____
_____
_____
_____
_____
_____
_____
_____
_____
_____
_____

## THINGS TO BE GRATEFUL FOR TODAY

Date:     /     /

_____
_____
_____
_____
_____
_____
_____
_____
_____
_____
_____
_____
_____
_____
_____
_____
_____
_____
_____
_____
_____
_____

## THINGS TO BE GRATEFUL FOR TODAY

Date:        /        /

_____

_____

_____

_____

_____

_____

_____

_____

_____

_____

_____

_____

_____

_____

_____

_____

_____

_____

_____

_____

_____

## THINGS TO BE GRATEFUL FOR TODAY

> *"Life isn't about finding yourself. Life is about creating yourself."* - George Bernard Shaw

Date:     /     /

_____

_____
_____
_____
_____
_____
_____
_____
_____
_____
_____
_____
_____
_____
_____
_____
_____
_____
_____
_____
_____

## THINGS TO BE GRATEFUL FOR TODAY

> *"Change your life today. Don't gamble on the future, act now, without delay."* — *Simone de Beauvoir*

Date:     /     /
_____

_____
_____
_____
_____
_____
_____
_____
_____
_____
_____
_____
_____
_____
_____
_____
_____
_____
_____
_____

## THINGS TO BE GRATEFUL FOR TODAY

Date:     /     /

THINGS TO BE GRATEFUL FOR TODAY

Date:        /        /

THINGS TO BE GRATEFUL FOR TODAY

*"When life gives you lemons, add a little gin and tonic"*

Date:     /     /

---

## THINGS TO BE GRATEFUL FOR TODAY

Date:       /       /

_____

_____

_____

_____

_____

_____

_____

_____

_____

_____

_____

_____

_____

_____

_____

_____

_____

_____

## THINGS TO BE GRATEFUL FOR TODAY

*"When you feel you are defeated, just remember,*
*you have the power to move on, it is all in your mind"*

Date:        /        /

THINGS TO BE GRATEFUL FOR TODAY

*"Don't just dream your dreams, make them happen!"*

Date:     /     /

THINGS TO BE GRATEFUL FOR TODAY

Date:    /    /

_____

_____

_____

_____

_____

_____

_____

_____

_____

_____

_____

_____

_____

_____

_____

_____

_____

_____

_____

_____

## THINGS TO BE GRATEFUL FOR TODAY

*"You are the creator of your own opportunities"*

Date:      /      /

_____
_____
_____
_____
_____
_____
_____
_____
_____
_____
_____
_____
_____
_____
_____
_____
_____
_____
_____

## THINGS TO BE GRATEFUL FOR TODAY

Date:      /      /

## THINGS TO BE GRATEFUL FOR TODAY

*"Success is not a place or a destination, it is a way of thinking while always having a new goal in mind"*

Date: / /

THINGS TO BE GRATEFUL FOR TODAY

Date:     /     /

_____

_____
_____
_____
_____
_____
_____
_____
_____
_____
_____
_____
_____
_____
_____
_____
_____
_____
_____
_____
_____

## THINGS TO BE GRATEFUL FOR TODAY

> *"Change the world one dream at a time, believe in your dreams"*

Date:      /     /

_____
_____
_____
_____
_____
_____
_____
_____
_____
_____
_____
_____
_____
_____
_____
_____
_____
_____
_____

## THINGS TO BE GRATEFUL FOR TODAY

*"Never loose confidence in your dreams, there will be obstacles and defeats, but you will always win if you persist"*

Date:      /     /

THINGS TO BE GRATEFUL FOR TODAY

Date:      /     /

THINGS TO BE GRATEFUL FOR TODAY

Date:      /      /

THINGS TO BE GRATEFUL FOR TODAY

*"Dreams make things happen, nothing is impossible as long as you believe."* - Anonymous

Date:     /     /

_____

_____
_____
_____
_____
_____
_____
_____
_____
_____
_____
_____
_____
_____
_____
_____
_____
_____
_____
_____

## THINGS TO BE GRATEFUL FOR TODAY

*"Always dream big and follow your heart"*

Date:      /      /

THINGS TO BE GRATEFUL FOR TODAY

Date:    /    /

## THINGS TO BE GRATEFUL FOR TODAY

Date:     /     /

THINGS TO BE GRATEFUL FOR TODAY

*"Dream big, it's the first step to success"* - Anonymous

Date:      /     /

_____
_____
_____
_____
_____
_____
_____
_____
_____
_____
_____
_____
_____
_____
_____
_____
_____
_____

## THINGS TO BE GRATEFUL FOR TODAY

> *"A successful person is someone that understands temporary defeat as a learning process, never give up!"*

Date:      /      /

_____

_____

_____

_____

_____

_____

_____

_____

_____

_____

_____

_____

_____

_____

_____

_____

_____

_____

## THINGS TO BE GRATEFUL FOR TODAY

> *"Motivation comes from working on our dreams and from taking action to achieve our goals"*

Date:      /      /

_____

_____

_____

_____

_____

_____

_____

_____

_____

_____

_____

_____

_____

_____

_____

_____

_____

_____

_____

## THINGS TO BE GRATEFUL FOR TODAY

> *"Dreams are the foundation to our imagination and success"*

Date:        /        /

_____

_____
_____
_____
_____
_____
_____
_____
_____
_____
_____
_____
_____
_____
_____
_____
_____
_____
_____

## THINGS TO BE GRATEFUL FOR TODAY

> *"Your mission in life should be to thrive and not merely survive"*

Date:     /     /

_____

_____
_____
_____
_____
_____
_____
_____
_____
_____
_____
_____
_____
_____
_____
_____
_____
_____
_____
_____

## THINGS TO BE GRATEFUL FOR TODAY

*"Doing what you believe in, and going after your dreams will only result in success."* - Anonymous

Date:     /     /

THINGS TO BE GRATEFUL FOR TODAY

*"The right time to start something new is now"*

Date:      /     /

THINGS TO BE GRATEFUL FOR TODAY

> *"Be brave, fight for what you believe in and make your dreams a reality."* - Anonymous

Date:      /    /

THINGS TO BE GRATEFUL FOR TODAY

Date:      /      /

_____

_____

_____

_____

_____

_____

_____

_____

_____

_____

_____

_____

_____

_____

_____

_____

_____

_____

_____

_____

## THINGS TO BE GRATEFUL FOR TODAY

> *"Let your dreams be bigger than your fears and your actions louder than your words." - Anonymous*

Date:     /     /

_____

_____
_____
_____
_____
_____
_____
_____
_____
_____
_____
_____
_____
_____
_____
_____
_____
_____
_____
_____
_____

## THINGS TO BE GRATEFUL FOR TODAY

*"Always keep moving forward to keep your balance, if you stop dreaming you will fall"*

Date:      /      /
_____
_____
_____
_____
_____
_____
_____
_____
_____
_____
_____
_____
_____
_____
_____
_____
_____
_____

## THINGS TO BE GRATEFUL FOR TODAY

Date:     /     /

_____

_____
_____
_____
_____
_____
_____
_____
_____
_____
_____
_____
_____
_____
_____
_____
_____
_____
_____

## THINGS TO BE GRATEFUL FOR TODAY

Date:      /      /

THINGS TO BE GRATEFUL FOR TODAY

Date:      /     /

## THINGS TO BE GRATEFUL FOR TODAY

*"If you have big dreams you will always have big reasons to wake up every day"*

Date:      /      /

_____

_____

_____

_____

_____

_____

_____

_____

_____

_____

_____

_____

_____

_____

_____

_____

_____

_____

## THINGS TO BE GRATEFUL FOR TODAY

*"Difficulties are nothing more than opportunities in disguise, keep on trying and you will succeed"*

Date:        /        /

---

## THINGS TO BE GRATEFUL FOR TODAY

Date:      /      /

_____

_____

_____

_____

_____

_____

_____

_____

_____

_____

_____

_____

_____

_____

_____

_____

_____

_____

## THINGS TO BE GRATEFUL FOR TODAY

*"Always have a powerful reason to wake up every new morning, set goals and follow your dreams"*

Date:      /      /

_____

_____
_____
_____
_____
_____
_____
_____
_____
_____
_____
_____
_____
_____
_____
_____
_____
_____
_____

## THINGS TO BE GRATEFUL FOR TODAY

*"Use failure as a motivation tool not as a sign of defeat"*

Date:        /        /

THINGS TO BE GRATEFUL FOR TODAY

*"Never let your dreams die for fear of failure, defeat is just temporary; your dreams are your power"*

Date:     /     /

## THINGS TO BE GRATEFUL FOR TODAY

> *"A failure is a lesson, not a loss. It is a temporary and sometimes necessary detour, not a dead end"*

Date:      /      /

THINGS TO BE GRATEFUL FOR TODAY

Date:      /      /

THINGS TO BE GRATEFUL FOR TODAY

Date:      /     /

THINGS TO BE GRATEFUL FOR TODAY

Date:      /      /

THINGS TO BE GRATEFUL FOR TODAY

> *"Never let your doubt blind your goals, for your future lies in your ability, not your failure"* — Anonymous

Date:     /     /

_____

_____

_____

_____

_____

_____

_____

_____

_____

_____

_____

_____

_____

_____

_____

_____

_____

## THINGS TO BE GRATEFUL FOR TODAY

*"Don't go into something to test the waters,
go into things to make waves"* — Anonymous

Date:      /      /

_____

_____
_____
_____
_____
_____
_____
_____
_____
_____
_____
_____
_____
_____
_____
_____
_____
_____
_____
_____

## THINGS TO BE GRATEFUL FOR TODAY

*"Laughter is the shock absorber that softens and minimizes the bumps of life"* — Anonymous

Date:     /     /

## THINGS TO BE GRATEFUL FOR TODAY

## "Dream – Believe – Achieve"

Date:  /  /
_____

_____
_____
_____
_____
_____
_____
_____
_____
_____
_____
_____
_____
_____
_____
_____
_____
_____
_____
_____
_____

## THINGS TO BE GRATEFUL FOR TODAY

> *"Make your own destiny. Don't wait for it to come to you, life is not a rehearsal"* — Anonymous

Date:     /     /

_____

_____
_____
_____
_____
_____
_____
_____
_____
_____
_____
_____
_____
_____
_____
_____
_____
_____
_____
_____
_____

## THINGS TO BE GRATEFUL FOR TODAY

> *"If you want to feel rich, just count all the things you have that money can't buy"* — *Anonymous*

Date:     /     /

## THINGS TO BE GRATEFUL FOR TODAY

*"Never give up on a dream just because of the time it will take to accomplish it. The time will pass anyway."* – Anonymous

Date: / /

___

## THINGS TO BE GRATEFUL FOR TODAY

*"I am never a failure until I begin blaming others"*
*- Anonymous*

Date:      /      /
_____

_____
_____
_____
_____
_____
_____
_____
_____
_____
_____
_____
_____
_____
_____
_____
_____
_____
_____

## THINGS TO BE GRATEFUL FOR TODAY

Date:      /     /

_____

_____

_____

_____

_____

_____

_____

_____

_____

_____

_____

_____

_____

_____

_____

_____

_____

_____

_____

_____

## THINGS TO BE GRATEFUL FOR TODAY

Date:     /     /

_____

_____
_____
_____
_____
_____
_____
_____
_____
_____
_____
_____
_____
_____
_____
_____
_____
_____
_____
_____

## THINGS TO BE GRATEFUL FOR TODAY

Date:     /     /

## THINGS TO BE GRATEFUL FOR TODAY

Date:      /      /

## THINGS TO BE GRATEFUL FOR TODAY

*"Never let defeat have the last word"* — Anonymous

Date:      /      /

_____

_____

_____

_____

_____

_____

_____

_____

_____

_____

_____

_____

_____

_____

_____

_____

## THINGS TO BE GRATEFUL FOR TODAY

Date:     /     /
_____
_____
_____
_____
_____
_____
_____
_____
_____
_____
_____
_____
_____
_____
_____
_____
_____
_____
_____
_____

## THINGS TO BE GRATEFUL FOR TODAY

> *"There is no elevator to success.*
> *You have to take the stairs"* — Anonymous

Date:    /    /

_____

_____

_____

_____

_____

_____

_____

_____

_____

_____

_____

_____

_____

_____

_____

_____

_____

_____

_____

_____

## THINGS TO BE GRATEFUL FOR TODAY

*"Don't let yesterday's disappointments, overshadow tomorrow's achievements"* — Anonymous

Date:     /     /

THINGS TO BE GRATEFUL FOR TODAY

Date:      /      /

_____

_____

_____

_____

_____

_____

_____

_____

_____

_____

_____

_____

_____

_____

_____

_____

## THINGS TO BE GRATEFUL FOR TODAY

Date:      /      /

_____

_____
_____
_____
_____
_____
_____
_____
_____
_____
_____
_____
_____
_____
_____
_____
_____
_____
_____
_____
_____

## THINGS TO BE GRATEFUL FOR TODAY

Date:        /        /

THINGS TO BE GRATEFUL FOR TODAY

Date:        /        /
_____

_____
_____
_____
_____
_____
_____
_____
_____
_____
_____
_____
_____
_____
_____
_____
_____
_____
_____

## THINGS TO BE GRATEFUL FOR TODAY

*"Try and fail, but don't fail to try"* — Anonymous

Date:      /      /

THINGS TO BE GRATEFUL FOR TODAY

Date:    /    /

THINGS TO BE GRATEFUL FOR TODAY

Date:      /      /

## THINGS TO BE GRATEFUL FOR TODAY

> *"No dreamer is ever too small; no dream is ever too big." – Anonymous*

Date:     /     /

_____

_____

_____

_____

_____

_____

_____

_____

_____

_____

_____

_____

_____

_____

_____

_____

_____

_____

## THINGS TO BE GRATEFUL FOR TODAY

*"All our tomorrows depend on today"* — *Anonymous*

Date: / /

_____

_____

_____

_____

_____

_____

_____

_____

_____

_____

_____

_____

_____

_____

_____

_____

_____

_____

_____

## THINGS TO BE GRATEFUL FOR TODAY

Date:    /    /

## THINGS TO BE GRATEFUL FOR TODAY

Date:      /      /

_____

_____
_____
_____
_____
_____
_____
_____
_____
_____
_____
_____
_____
_____
_____
_____
_____
_____
_____
_____

## THINGS TO BE GRATEFUL FOR TODAY

> *"Don't be pushed by your problems.*
> *Be led by your dreams"* — Anonymous

Date:    /    /

_____
_____
_____
_____
_____
_____
_____
_____
_____
_____
_____
_____
_____
_____
_____
_____
_____
_____

## THINGS TO BE GRATEFUL FOR TODAY

Date:     /     /

_____

_____

_____

_____

_____

_____

_____

_____

_____

_____

_____

_____

_____

_____

_____

_____

_____

_____

## THINGS TO BE GRATEFUL FOR TODAY

Date:        /      /

_____

_____

_____

_____

_____

_____

_____

_____

_____

_____

_____

_____

_____

_____

_____

_____

_____

_____

## THINGS TO BE GRATEFUL FOR TODAY

Date:      /      /

_____

_____

_____

_____

_____

_____

_____

_____

_____

_____

_____

_____

_____

_____

_____

_____

_____

_____

_____

## THINGS TO BE GRATEFUL FOR TODAY

> *"You create your life by following your dreams with decisive actions"*

Date: / /

_____

_____

_____

_____

_____

_____

_____

_____

_____

_____

_____

_____

_____

_____

_____

_____

_____

_____

## THINGS TO BE GRATEFUL FOR TODAY

Date:        /        /

THINGS TO BE GRATEFUL FOR TODAY

*"Difficult roads often lead to beautiful destinations"*

Date:      /      /

THINGS TO BE GRATEFUL FOR TODAY

> *"The road to success is always full of surprises and temporary failures, real success comes to those who persist"*

Date:    /    /

_____

_____

_____

_____

_____

_____

_____

_____

_____

_____

_____

_____

_____

_____

_____

_____

_____

_____

_____

## THINGS TO BE GRATEFUL FOR TODAY

## "Believe in yourself and you will be unstoppable"

Date:     /     /

_____

_____

_____

_____

_____

_____

_____

_____

_____

_____

_____

_____

_____

_____

_____

_____

_____

## THINGS TO BE GRATEFUL FOR TODAY

Date:     /     /

_____
_____
_____
_____
_____
_____
_____
_____
_____
_____
_____
_____
_____
_____
_____
_____
_____

## THINGS TO BE GRATEFUL FOR TODAY

Date:      /      /

## THINGS TO BE GRATEFUL FOR TODAY

Date:      /      /

_____

_____

_____

_____

_____

_____

_____

_____

_____

_____

_____

_____

_____

_____

_____

_____

_____

_____

_____

## THINGS TO BE GRATEFUL FOR TODAY

Date:       /      /

## THINGS TO BE GRATEFUL FOR TODAY

Date:      /     /

THINGS TO BE GRATEFUL FOR TODAY

Date:      /      /

_____

_____
_____
_____
_____
_____
_____
_____
_____
_____
_____
_____
_____
_____
_____
_____
_____
_____
_____

## THINGS TO BE GRATEFUL FOR TODAY

Date:      /      /

THINGS TO BE GRATEFUL FOR TODAY

Date:    /    /

## THINGS TO BE GRATEFUL FOR TODAY

Date:        /        /

THINGS TO BE GRATEFUL FOR TODAY

Date:      /      /

THINGS TO BE GRATEFUL FOR TODAY

Date:     /     /

_____
_____
_____
_____
_____
_____
_____
_____
_____
_____
_____
_____
_____
_____
_____
_____
_____
_____
_____
_____

## THINGS TO BE GRATEFUL FOR TODAY

Date:      /      /

_____

_____

_____

_____

_____

_____

_____

_____

_____

_____

_____

_____

_____

_____

_____

_____

_____

## THINGS TO BE GRATEFUL FOR TODAY

**CREATIVE JOURNALS**
**FACTORY**

We hope you liked your journal – notebook,
please let us know if you liked it by writing a
review, it means a lot to us.

*Thank you!*

**DESIGNED BY POSITIVE GIFTS PRESS FOR:**

**CREATIVE JOURNALS FACTORY**

FIND OTHER BEAUTIFUL JOURNALS, DIARIES AND NOTEBOOKS AT:

JOURNALS - DIARIES - NOTEBOOKS - COLORING BOOKS

Made in the USA
Monee, IL
27 May 2021